**"BEIGE is the texture of stucco,** the beach and the body shops, the early school shootings, the sound of the crickets, the new tracts of 5000 square-foot middle-class homes in east San Diego. BEIGE results from Porcari's and Mori's long friendship. The pulse of their book beats like a hummingbird's heart."

**—Chris Kraus**

**"Perhaps there's no wisdom in the banal,** but perhaps some wisdom in looking at the limits of wisdom, at beige as tonal standard, at things mute in their thingness—dreams of things, perhaps, things dreaming of themselves—that lie outside of 'wisdom'. Bruna Mori conjures wit and wry tenderness in the interplay between her language and George Porcari's full frontal quintessential Southern California landscapes. The last time you were asked your favorite color, you didn't say this, but clearly more than we suspected, Beige is fun!"

**—Sesshu Foster**

**Bruna Mori**       **George Porcari**

**UpSet Press**
PO Box 200340
Brooklyn, NY 11220
**www.upsetpress.org**

Established in 2000, UpSet Press is an independent, not-for-profit (501c3 tax-exempt) press based in Brooklyn. The original impetus of the press was to upset the status quo through art and literature. The Press has expanded its mission to promote new work by new authors; the first works, or complete works, of established authors—placing a special emphasis on restoring to print new editions of exceptional texts; and first time translations of works into English. Overall, UpSet Press endeavors to advance artists' innovative visions and works that engender new directions in art and literature.

**Creative direction and design**
Jessica D'Elena-Tweed

**Design production**
Karen Davison

**Some words**
Lucien Mori Darini Bratton

Photo credit, page 74: Image captured by Dr. Chris A. Martin, Professor of Horticulture, Arizona State University.

Library of Congress Control Number: 2018959333
ISBN 978-1-937357-81-8
Printed in the United States of America

"WHEN THE FAIRY PRINCESS  LEFT THE CASTLE WALLS SHE MADE IT AS FAR AS         THE LOCAL 7-11
BUT AT LEAST THAT WAS BETTER THAN NOWHERE."


—AKILAH OLIVER

**Approximate beige**

**Mustard beige**

**Gardena beige**

Hustler Casino beige

Beige beige

beige

As if a world begins,
hills houses.

There is no map or

YOU
ARE
HERE

-type directory on
view in the lobby.

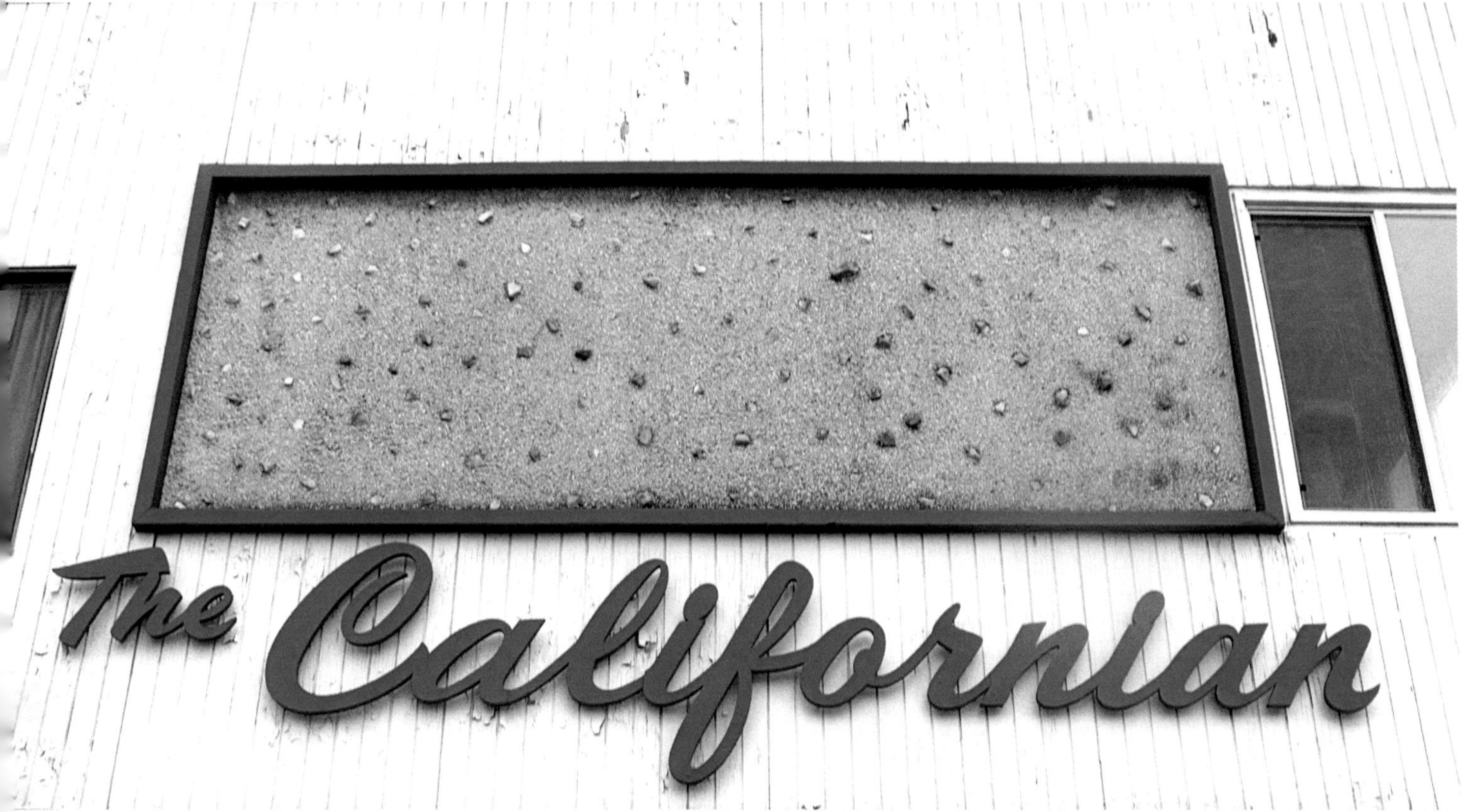
The Californian

Blue trellis

A close beach

'50s sign repainted late '70s

1
5
2
0

Cemented

There are two apartments for rent
in The Californian (as opposed to The Suburban)

Look hard at this flatness that somehow
heightens the children's run as highway
meridians sprout homes as clay grey as
this border of divider and sky.

*"Is the ocean        this way        or this way?                "*

PRIVATE
PARKING
FOR
RICH'S
CARPET

STORE HOURS
MONDAY THROUGH FRIDAY
9 TO 11:30
CLOSED 2 HOURS
BACK 1:30 TO 5
SATURDAY 9 TO 5
SUNDAY CLOSED

Parking reserved

for Rev. Shindo only

**Remember when you were little and I took you**

I said to look at the python, not an insect, but you were staring at

**to insect day sponsored by a pest control**

the common fruit fly. Then there was an owl there, too, trying to

**company. And the mix of magnifying glasses**

sleep, because it's nocturnal, and millipedes crawled up your arm.

**and fly swatters was very confusing.**

REMEMBER WHEN THAT SATANIST FRIEND
OF A FRIEND SHOWED UP TO YOUR 33RD
BIRTHDAY AND THEN ON EASTER WE RAN
INTO HIM AND KENNETH ANGER.

Remember that before you knew
he was a Satanist, you went to visit
him when you discovered he lived
nearby, in that apartment across from the halfway house.

And he showed you the Argento film, the one with Asia in it. Then he made a pass at you, and you said you didn't think of him that way, though he tried to find some meaning in coincidence.

**It is
"The World's Biggest Lemon."**

There is a ten-foot-wide statue of a lemon located at 3361 Main Street. It sits near a small lemon grove beside the local Trolley station and downtown bus stop. Written across the base of this monument is "Best Climate on Earth."

The grid is a compass of possibility.
A meat market next to a dog groomer
seems like a bad idea. Cars have about
a minute wait before the light turns
on the corner of Lemon Grove Avenue
and Broadway.

I google Baskin Robbins to see if it is still there; the last time it was
Yelped was 2009, and it was reviewed as "being sticky."

Someone wrote: "I think it is a Haagen Daaz now." When I go, in fact,
it is called Maggie's and they sell Dreyer's ice cream. I am told it is
co-owned by the guy who founded Icicles, whatever that means.

S
T

At Maggie's, they serve up to five customers at a time. Cellular automata. How bodies go or never arrive.

"I used to work here when I was about your age, you know,"

I say to the 16-year-old cashier.

"Oh."

A particular sound marked the boundary
of the neighborhood. It was the roosters
near full dark in the summer.

Do you remember them? The flat cockle-doodle
wafted up, unhinged from causes—not necessarily
your neighbor's rooster but their rooster, too.
That sound became the whole neighborhood clearing
its throat before going to bed and then waking.

*The yellow-beige calm of succulents.*
*The faded flamingo. The burnt-out angel.*
*And two very small corpses.*

TWO LEMON GROVE TEENAGERS VENTURED INTO CAVES NEAR CHIHUAHUA, MEXICO IN 1966 IN SEARCH OF A MUMMY. THE TEENS FINALLY FOUND TWO, A GIRL AND AN INFANT, WHICH THEY PACKED UP AND SMUGGLED ACROSS THE BORDER.

For 14 years, the mummies remained in a Lemon Grove garage until someone happened to clean it out and discover them, leading the community to believe a murder had taken place. The mummies were not returned but now reside in The San Diego Museum of Man, though they are not San Diegans,

*-nor men.*

Eric made beautiful
posters of
**"*NO BUSINESS
AS USUAL DAY*"**
for a rally in the eighties—
one where they threw
bricks through storefronts.
The final image was a
series of smiley faces
transforming to atomic
bombs, with a hand
tearing apart the scene.

Years later, I saw it in a graphic design coffee table book in a high-end boutique that was probably worthy of a brick.

is just doing what he needs to do.

# SPIDER-MAN

The five year old points his gun at me.

Then asks his dad, "Where's mom?"

"We're a little further down the road than we thought."

sometimes pirates fight for necklaces
there is no peace in fighting it's just part
of life and it's okay to lie at magic camp
but if the world breaks now it's made there
will be blood beneath the street blood
looks like hot lava shining in the sunlight
the food store has run out of batteries and
luck $_o$ur faces d$_o$n't match

dear lucien,

bored paint brush through socks

that boogie looks like a song too
the bow with the needle that is t
rainbow's colors touch the groun
except the clouds,

lucien

night, organ palettes

is the day with the ribbon or
eaded and shot but doesn't hurt
hite is for everything else,

(this is like a jellyfish puffing) loving yourself is importantest for you your heart is very expensive

someday i'll come back to you in my racecar

Two Secret Service men were sitting on my mother's ~~orange~~ xxxxxxxx couch wearing ~~grey~~ xxxxx suits in one-hundred-degree heat.

I had come in from the public pool and was wearing ~~red~~ swim trunks, a ~~yellow~~ xxxxxxx towel around my neck and bright ~~blue~~ xxxx flip flops.

My mother spoke for me and
explained that I would never write
a letter to President Johnson
threatening to kill him.

I sat down across from them on
a plastic dining room chair with
~~blue~~ and ~~green~~ flower prints.

—They say you wrote a letter . . . to President Johnson . . .

saying he should be killed because of the war in Viet-Nam!


—How do you feel about the war?

The older man asked the question as if he knew the answer.

He resembled Eisenhower from the photographs of him just after that other war, and the younger man looked exactly like John Glenn, the American astronaut that had only recently traveled in space.

**The m^o on landing was two years away.**

The principal, whom we had nicknamed Bluebeard, ran against us toward a shooting asking what had happened, but no one stopped to answer him. We all just pointed in the same direction with our mouths open.

The boy survived, and the man who fired the shot was found to have been double crossed in a scheme to steal money from the local Taco Bell.

**Mr. Bartel taught photography**
showing us how to print negatives, how
use a camera, how to measure time in
fractions of seconds, how to arrange a
still life so it conformed to something
called "the golden mean" that all great
artists from the past used.

He emphasized that it was available to everyone "democratically", that **this golden mean is within your means.**

Men who flunked every class they had could spot the kind of car and the year from just a glance at the corner of a fender.

We spoke the argot of the farm because our parents were immigrants from small towns in states that we had never

seen such as Wyoming and South Dakota and Michigan.

I had come the farthest being from Peru—I was always explaining where Peru was and it seemed that to some

the very concept of South America was so other worldly that there was not much to say after that.

# ROADIUM

OPEN AIR MARKET

OPEN
AIR
RKET

At night we would go climb the trees
near the Roadium Drive-In Theatre
where they showed adult films after 10.

From the trees
you couldn't hear anything but
the sound of crickets and the traffic of
Redondo Beach Boulevard
which was six lanes wide and full of

used car lots

fast food take-out stands

gas stations

tire stores

banks and

apartment buildings

with names like Pacifica and Kahuna.

I still remember a sequence from one of the films I saw
   at the Roadium: a dark-haired woman enters
a house wearing a full-lenth fur coat which she takes off
   revealing she is naked. As she throws the fur
   to the floor, she opens her arms and throws herself
               on the one who has opened the door.

*Lynda!*

**George?** *Oh my God! What are you doing here?*

`Nothing much. How about you?`

*I'm okay. You remember me?*

`Of course I remember. Lynda with a 'y.'`
`Can't forget that ever.`

*I'm just working here for now until something better comes along.*

We said more in a mall in 10 minutes than we ever had and
ever would, and it wasn't that much.

I still dressed like a kid with tennis shoes and blue jeans
that were too big for me, and a shirt that my mother had chosen.

**What is the working title?**

*BEIGE*.

**What is the one sentence synopsis?**

There is no wisdom of the banal, just the smell of bougainvillea.

**Where did the idea for this project come from?**

Bruna saw George's show at Cottage Home gallery in L.A. They discussed the prospect of pairing his photos with her text for on a chapbook. It began as a transcript of a McDonald's drive-thru called *May I Take Your Order*, then grew into a treatise on the suburbs called *BEIGE*.

**What inspired BEIGE?**

George and Bruna wanted to revisit the places they first landed when they
moved to California (suburban Gardena in the sixties via Lima, Peru,
and suburban San Diego in the eighties via New Orleans, Upstate New York,
and Kyushu, Japan).

**How will the collaboration be shown or published?**

*BEIGE* was hung at La Esquina in San Diego in conjunction with a class
on suburban drifts at UC San Diego and Woodbury School of Architecture;
presented at the La Jolla Historical Society, San Diego Museum of Art for
Agitprop Gallery, Little Tokyo Design Week, and Hop Louie for Tif Sigfrids
gallery; and excerpted in Night Papers (Night Gallery).

**How long did it take to make the first draft?**

One day for *May I Take Your Order*. Five years for *BEIGE*.

The above was first published in LACE Gallery's CLOSER blog (Los Angeles) for #thenextbigthing.

## MORI

**Bruna Mori** is a writer and educator, preoccupied with spatial discourses. Born in Japan, she moved itinerantly, yet keeps landing back in the San Diego suburbs. Her books are *Poetry for Corporations* (Insert Blanc Press, 2019) and *Dérive* (Meritage Press, 2006). She has published numerous articles, essays, and chapbooks, and taught poetics at the University of California, San Diego, California Institute of the Arts, Southern California Institute of Architecture, and Art Center College of Design. Her MFA and BA degrees were completed at Bard College and the University of California, San Diego.

## PORCARI

**George Porcari** is an artist and photographer based in Los Angeles. Born in Peru, George emigrated to Gardena, California in the sixties and began his lifelong vocation in observing and documenting his surroundings. Porcari attended Pratt Institute and Art Center College of Design, where he has also taught film and collage history classes and worked as an acquisitions librarian for many years. He has exhibited widely and internationally since 1988; his most recent solo exhibitions were at Haphazard Gallery, Tif's Desk, and China Art Objects. His numerous critical essays and other writings have appeared in such places as *CINEAction*, *NY arts*, and *Inflatable Magazine*. He occasionally revisits the suburbs.